BIKERS

LEGEND, LEGACY AND LIFE

Published in 2002 by
INDEPENDENT MUSIC PRESS

Independent Music Press is an imprint of I.M.P. Publishing Ltd

Bikers: Legend, Legacy And Life
by Gary Charles

British Library Cataloguing-in-Publication Data.
A catalogue for this book is available from The British Library.

Cover photograph by Gareth Brown
Internal photographs by Barry Love and Stephen Stratton
Editorial Assistant to Gary Charles: Simon Culleton

ISBN 0-9539942-2-8
1 2 3 4 5 6 7 8 9 10

Printed in the UK.

INDEPENDENT MUSIC PRESS

P.O. Box 14691, London, SE1 2ZA
Fax: 01440 788 562

For a free catalogue, e-mail us at:
info@impbooks.com

Visit us on the web at: www.impbooks.com

Bikers:
Legend, Legacy and Life

by Gary Charles

Independent Music Press
London

For all the Bros who have been taken from us.
May they *never* be forgotten and may they
always be in our thoughts riding free...

Bikers: Legend, Legacy & Life

Contents:

Foreword

Live to Ride
Ride to Live!

I own a motorbike. Big deal, you may say, and you'd be right. But I own a motorbike, NOT a motorcycle. The difference? To the untutored nothing. But to the lifestyle riders among you, plenty. The difference is in what the machine means to its respective owner: what ultimately the person behind the bars believes his (or her) steed stands for. Why? Read on and all will be revealed as I take you on an adrenalin pumping pit-stop tour of the world's largest yet most misunderstood motorised culture ever: a culture which, as we sit in the first quarter of a new century, has a heritage spanning back to the middle of the last. Before we enter that world though, my credentials.

As stated I own a motorbike. It is not an all-singing all-dancing fibreglass faired ankles-up-your-arse racer, but a big mean-looking piece of glossy black equipment. It is not particularly pretty, nor is it ugly. It is however all paid for, road legal and mine. And that's all I'm going to say about it, as its make and original model details (yes, it has been altered from factory standard) are no one's business but my own - especially as some may question my impartiality when commenting on other marques should its make and model become known.

I have owned an array of two (and occasionally three) wheeled vehicles over the many years that have lapsed since my Secondary schooling ended, and although all these machines have provided transport (to varying degrees of comfort and reliability), this facet has usually been an additional consideration over and above each machine's cultural status. I have worked and lived in both the north and south of England. I have lived and worked in America for a motorbike outlet, and have spent more years than I care to comment on as an oily engineer. I have ridden two wheels across Europe on numerous occasions and cruised a Harley-Davidson down Highway 101 in the Californian sun.

I have had some fantastic times astride my machines, and some which were frankly appalling. While riding I have felt the wind in my hair, the sun on my back and stinging rain on my face. I have experienced being both hot and cold aboard a bike, and have found and lost love through the same. I have made some truly golden friends through two-wheeled camaraderie, but have also felt the hurt and desperation of losing far too many of them through tragic accidents.

I have been hospitalised myself as the result of traffic accidents, and have witnessed things on the street best left unsaid. Thanks to the inspiration of the late Dr Maz Harris PhD of the Hells Angels MC, England, I also elected to enter Higher Education ten or so years ago as a (very) mature student studying the sociological and historical phenomena of 'vehicle-orientated sub-culture' for which I was awarded a Bachelor of Arts Degree. I have therefore lived, tasted and studied all aspects of life from the saddle and, as such, believe myself well placed to write the following chronicle. So read on, and experience - or re-live - this all-consuming and unique revolutionary way of life...

However, one more thing before I start - an apology. I apologise that this book will be, by necessity, a quick pit-stop tour of Biker culture, legend, legacy and life. I am sorry for the fleeting insights into areas which truly deserved more expansion, such as the ever-changing custom cycle scene. I apologise for the brief coverage of back patch clubs, but felt this best left at a level commensurate with existing common knowledge and/or information available on the internet out of respect for their privacy. I am similarly sorry for the hurried way in which we will bounce through the 1970s, 80s and 90s to the 21st Century. I acknowledge the numerous omissions that many of you may note, such as the non-mention of MAG (Motorcycle Action Group) who came to prominence in the UK after the compulsory wearing of crash-helmets was introduced in 1973, the NCC (National Chopper Club) and the non-mention of the 59 CLUB and CMCC (Christian Motorcycle Club). I don't apologise for not mentioning drugs however, as although many Bikers have used/use various forms of these (predominantly cannabis, speed and/or cocaine), as indeed have I, drugs have never been an integral part of Biking, merely a non-descript bolt-on that can be found in all walks of life.

There are good reasons for all the omissions however, not least that in an ideal world this book would be a précis of an ever-expanding part work covering many volumes. My primary concern as the author was to ensure that the areas I believed most relevant were represented, and covered in a way which sign-posted subjects worthy of further investigation by those who may wish to do so. This I hope I achieved. For those of you who do choose to investigate further, please see the bibliography at the end of this book.

Many of you may also take issue with the number of photographs used. However, the photos chosen have been carefully selected for their imagery, and are as integral a part of this title as the words themselves. If you'd rather see less text and more pictures, tough. After all, if it's pictures you want, subscribe to a Biker magazine. In fact do this anyway, as these mags are always a good read, and can keep you up to speed. Right then, let's move on.

chapter one:

Evolution
of
the
Species

When trying to trace the worldwide historical roots of lifestyle cult biking, putting information in any form of order poses a multitude of problems. Not least where do you focus: America or Britain? There is a good argument for both. Although documented examples of American motorbike gangs doing a bunch of American motorbike gang stuff pre-date those of their British counterparts (more about that later), Britain is the place I shall focus on first, as it was among the green leafy lanes of said fortress islands that I first encountered cult biking. Besides, Britain was the place where (arguably) the first identifiable and interconnected youth culture image galvanised en-masse (although it must be noted that when this happened, American influences were of paramount importance).

Teddy Boys & The Arrival of The Teenager

Until the end of World War II, British adolescents were thought of as either children or young adults, with no period of transition between. By the 1950s, however, growing economics and increased transatlantic awareness had a dramatic effect on this status quo. Due to Britain's (then) national labour shortage, fifteen-year-old British school leavers were gaining well-paid employment. This resulted in a surplus of cash in many youngsters' pockets after paying their housekeeping, with which they could do whatever they wanted (within reason). Couple this with having an eighteen month period of compulsory National Military Service hanging over them[1], and this left the males involved wanting plenty. They wanted to make the most of the limited civilian time they had available to them before the call of Queen and Country, and wanted to quite literally 'seize the day'. Thus the so-called 'teenage consumer' had been born, and society as it was would never be the same again.

This teenage phenomenon quickly attracted attention. A consultant psychiatrist concluded on 1950s BBC radio that "at adolescence, most people begin to feel very insecure. They are neither children nor adults and are not sure of themselves. Therefore, they get together in gangs of people with a similar outlook and that helps them to build up their confidence." How right she was. I will now quote a passage from another author whose interpretation and understanding of these events is, in my opinion, so factually correct that I could not improve on this myself.

"Right across the class spectrum, young people had been dressed as - and expected to behave as - slightly smaller versions of their parents, but now the concept of the teenager was emerging with a new and very distinct identity. These teenage fashion followers came primarily from the lower classes, as the upper-middle and upper classes preserved a 'hold' over their offspring for much longer.

Teenagers expressed their boredom and dissatisfaction with the clothes and music of their parents' generation and started to look to the USA for inspiration. To their great delight they found many influences, including early Rock & Roll. Not only was this music lively, exciting and completely new, but it had an added attraction; the collective and vehement disapproval of their parents which, of course, made it all the more seductive. Rock & Roll's meteoric rise in popularity was inevitable. Its wide-spread appeal was seen by adults and the totally adult-orientated media as reaching epidemic proportions among young people throughout the Western World.

The style of dress adopted by these early followers of British teenage fashion also became firmly fixed in the new Rock & Roll movement, but took their influence from the Edwardian period almost as a pastiche of (then) current upper-class dress. The males wore tight 'drainpipe' trousers, longer than usual jackets with trimmed collars and cuffs (called Drape coats because of their cut), elaborate waistcoats, string ties, pointed-toe boots (called winkle-pickers) or crepe-soled suede shoes (called brothel creepers), and greased their hair back into elaborate quiffs. This look originated completely in the UK. The females on the other hand wore the American-style full circular calf-length skirts, with their hair either up in a 'Beehive' style, or in a long pony-tail sprouting from their crown. These fashion conscious teenagers were graced courtesy of the press with the collective name Teddy Boys, Teddy Girls, or simply Teds. Such nicknames were derived fairly obviously from the abbreviations of Edward or Edwardian. These names stuck.

The Teddy Boy cult seems overly gaudy nowadays, and in many ways gauche, but it was the first true teenage cult. They needed to stand out from the crowd and advertise the arrival of the new face of adolescence. In the eyes of the general public however, this was seen as the birth of juvenile delinquency." (Gareth Brown: Scooter Boys *6th edition. Independent Music Press 2001. First published 1989).*

* * *

The public hysteria surrounding the Teddy Boys further thickened on the night of 23rd July 1956. Following a high level of youth popularity in the US of A, the film *Rock Around The Clock* opened at the Trocadero Cinema situated in London's Elephant and Castle region. In this film, the Rock & Roll legend Bill Haley and his band The Comets perform the title track, a song they first performed in an earlier film entitled *Concrete Jungle*. The following day's national British press reported that all hell broke loose as soon as the sound of 'Rock Around The Clock' (which by then had become something of an anthem) started to boom through the theatre. Ushers and cinema staff had to (allegedly) run for their lives, or so the press would have us believe.

Although the Trocadero did undeniably experience a degree of damage with some seat slashing with cut-throat razors (the Teddy Boys' purported favourite weapon, alongside polished brass knuckle-dusters), there wasn't any real civil unrest, just an outbreak of spontaneity. For the music inspired those present to move their feet and dance. Boys and girls, girls and girls, and even boys and boys started to jive in the cinema aisles, while some males even climbed on stage and started to do 'The Hop' (an intricate foot-flicking heel and toe dance and a step which is today vividly associated with true Rock & Roll dancing). Where sporadic incidents of Teddy Boy-inspired public disorder and gang violence did break out in the late 1950s, which it undeniably did, the causes were more than likely the bottled up frustrations and resentments felt by these emerging Teenagers towards the existing society of the day and possibly a restrictive fear of pending national service as mentioned, rather than out of a blatant disregard for people and property.

Rightly or wrongly, for the rest of that year, newspaper columnists reported again and again on the outrageous antics of the Teddy Boy (and Girl), and Dance Halls the length and breadth of Britain tried unsuccessfully to ban not only the Edwardian garb these youths had adopted, but also the music which fuelled them. Sinisterly, questions were asked in the House of Commons and, perhaps most bizarrely, Baden Powell tried to integrate the Teddy Boy into the Scouting movement (dib dib 'rocka' dob). But due to a mixture of commercialism (Rock & Roll was making a lot of people in the entertainment industry a lot of money), and the increased cache and appeal of this lifestyle, such sanctions failed miserably. Indeed, they served only to ensure that the fierce cultural pride of the youths of this era would last a lifetime. By way of example, fast forward to mid-November 2000, the scene of a Teddy Boy Rock & Roll reunion weekend held at Great Yarmouth in Norfolk, England. The event was attended by around 3000 drape coat-wearing individuals who Rocked and Rolled from Friday through - although it must be noted that for most, the only thing 'teenage' about them was the age of their great-grandchildren.

So there you have it, the emergence of the Teenager and the Teddy Boy. From these acorns mighty oaks would inevitably grow, sub-divide and prosper as we move onwards to the Ton-Up Boy: the foundling father of the British Biker. To conclude this section however, here is a list of five musical standards, in no particular order of importance, to remind you of the golden age that was Rock & Roll (note the deliberate exclusion of the trite and bubble-gum tune 'Leader of the Pack' by the 'Shangri-Las').[2]

'Rock Around The Clock' by Bill Haley & The Comets.
'Summertime Blues' by Eddie Cochran.
'Peggy Sue' by Buddy Holly & The Crickets.
'At The Hop' by Danny & The Juniors.
'Blue Suede Shoes' by Elvis Presley.

*Footnote 1
National Service had to be completed some time between their 18th and 26th birthday at the Government's discretion. National Service was not abolished in Britain until 1963.

*Footnote 2
As an appendix to the above account, and in order to air one of my major-league pet hates, it must be noted that the music mentioned

and listened to by the Teds was Rock & Roll and NOT one of the advancing derivatives from the 1960s through to now.

Admittedly many sub-divisional names have evolved to categorise the varying changes in style of emerging guitar-based music over the decades such as Rhythm & Blues and Heavy Metal (both of which shall be returned to later) and admittedly there are a number of contemporary bands who do record and perform traditional Rock & Roll. However, Rock & Roll should NOT be used as an umbrella term to encompass other forms of music. It is far too important a musical term to be degraded in this way, and far too important to have its historical context damaged. The reason why I stress this is because many misguided journalists (and a multitude of media-hyped performers) continually refer to ALL guitar-based bands as being Rock & Roll. WRONG! Rock they may be but Rock & Roll? NEVER!

The Rock & Roll sound is firmly fixed to the 50s. All else is 'something else' (as Eddie Cochran would say). As for the arse I heard on MTV referring to The Beatles (who most definitely weren't) and The Jackson Five (get real) as Rock & Roll... words fail me (or at least the printable ones do).

Right, enough said. Enter the Motorbike.

Ton-Up Boys & Cafe Racers

At the same time as the aforementioned Teenager phenomenon was exploding in the UK (and beyond), the British motorcycle industry was enjoying an almost unprecedented prosperity both at home and overseas. The marque of Triumph was particularly buoyant, boasting such luminaries among its riders as the Rock & Roll Legend Buddy Holly. American actor Marlon Brando would also come to enhance Triumph's twin cylinder motorcycles by riding an example of such in the film *The Wild One*, but more - much more - about that later.

In fact, from the 1930s onward, British motorcycles were so popular at home that marques such as Triumph, Norton, BSA, AJS, Matchless, Greaves, Brough, Vincent, Ariel, Douglas and Rudge (to list but a few) became household names. Stateside the same was happening for the motorcycle manufacturing companies of Indian and Harley-Davidson (the latter of which would in time come to dominate an important area of the worldwide lifestyle Biker scene) but as with every reference to the USA to date, more about that further on.

The reasoning behind the initial popularity of the motorcycle among the people of the post-war West was simple: transport. Compared to cars, motorcycles were cheap. They could be maintained with a degree of relative ease (unlike the high-tech guided missile motor bikes of the 21st century), and thanks to the emerging trend of hire purchase, were instantly available for the working man in a range of prices and specifications. They also came in an array of engine sizes ranging from the 98cc James (one of many small bikes manufactured by companies using proprietary brand engines from the likes of Villiers), up to the awesomely powerful (then and now) 1000cc Vincent Black Shadow. Supported by an equally vibrant used/second-hand machine market, 1950s Britain saw motorcycles truly mobilise the masses. Many Teds, too, turned to two wheels for transport at that time, although the standard status of the bikes they elected to ride was nothing more than a very basic blueprint for the aspiring road culture they would ultimately create.

During the 1950s, British motorcycles were winning racing trophies the world over, as indeed they had been doing for decades. As with the majority of young men then and now, the teenagers of 1950s Britain and America were mesmerised by the allure of speed. So if they wanted a motorbike, the chances were that they wanted it to look like one of the (then) state-of-the-art racing machines. However, this created a dilemma. Many a man had a motorcycle for transport at that time, so it was vital that the anti-establishment youths who acquired two-wheeled stallions ensured their bikes stood out from those of their fathers – for Teddy Boys in particular, blending into the crowd was a big taboo. Race replicas were not commercially available as stock items at that time though, so if such a machine was required, it had to be individually crafted.

Firstly, a suitable donor motorcycle had to be acquired. It was important that the blank canvas bike had a serious engine - favourites being 500cc machines and up. To achieve the racer look, its standard 'sit up and beg' handle bars would be removed, and lower or straight bars, drop angled Ace bars or proper racing clip-on bars would be installed in their place to enable the rider to hunch over the front of his steed in the same aerodynamic manner as the racing riders of the day. Exhausts would be modified to (arguably) increase performance - although invariably this did little more than enable the motors to make more noise - and where possible, streamlined aluminium petrol tanks would replace stock items and be polished to a dazzling gleam. Race-replica front-end bikini and full fairings were also introduced on occasion, but didn't really catch on in the mainstream, probably due to availability and cost. Engine tuning was also embraced by all to varying degrees, as almost everyone knew someone who could do a little 'tweaking' of essential bits and bobs. More often than not though, the owner/rider themselves would attempt this tuning (with varying degrees of success), as this was, and is, FUN!

Coupled with the adrenalin-inspiring exhilaration of actually riding the bike, playing with the engines in this way was one of the ultimate draws of the motorcycle to these emerging cult motorcyclists, as they could tinker with their toys to their heart's content. As a large proportion of the bikes modified in this way were aged and incontinent with oil leakages etc, to do either of the above resulted unavoidably in oil-stained and splattered clothing. For the fashion conscious and immaculately presented Ted, this raised a *serious* problem.

Exacerbating these concerns was another very real aspect of riding a motorbike, namely it is not if you fall off but when. If the rider constantly flirts with disaster by speeding as fast as possible for as long as possible, which these pioneering cult motorcyclists began to do, pre-planning and preparing for such an unwanted inevitability was of the utmost importance. This in mind, it became all too apparent to the Teddy Boy that the fine fabric of an Edwardian suit would not keep an abrasive road surface at bay for long in the event of an accident, and that ultimately should such a scenario occur, their flesh would very quickly be ripped to shreds. Inevitably, protective leather clothing started to enter the wardrobe of the motorcycling teenage Ted. Simultaneously, certain facets of Ted fashion started to enter the wardrobes of the non-Ted. So born out of an important practicality, a new amalgamated image started to emerge centred around young British Rock & Rollers, with the added inspiration of the motorcycle and leather. Although this image had to necessarily incorporate items worn by the older two-wheeled enthusiasts, through adaptation and attitude these new riders would always be easily distinguishable from their father's generation, for ever and ever Amen.

Selective surplus military clothing formed the basics of the protective uniform worn by these road racing recruits, and incorporated such items as sheep-skin -lined Air Force pilot jackets, reinforced glass flying goggles and army motorcycle despatch rider boots (all of which still enjoy a degree of popularity today). The tan sleeveless jerkins worn by WWII Allied despatch riders however (a thick hide knee-length leather waist-coat worn over the top of other outer garments for protection) were left in the surplus stores for the 'transport only' motorcyclists, as these were thought too 'un-cool' for the image conscious motorised teenage tearaways of Britain, America and Germany (where by the late 1950s similar things were starting to happen).

The sartorial ensemble was completed by heavyweight denim jeans tucked into long white socks which in turn had to be folded back over the tops of the boots to give an inch wide band. This subtle subversion showed that born out of an essential practicality and need for protection, a cult motorcycle image had found its infancy.

Not wanting to miss an opportunity, it wasn't too long before the leather tanners that already produced certain staid items of motorcycle wear for Mr and Mrs Sensible started to make and market a more refined range of apparel aimed at these youngsters. This helped spread the look, as supply and demand dictated a market trend which in turn created consumer want: a facet of youth culture which - be it good, bad, or indifferent - still endures to this day.

Although crash-helmets were not compulsory anywhere in the world during this period, for many cult Bikers they were slowly becoming acceptable - again most likely born out of a practical need for protection. These were not the full-face fibreglass items associated with 21st century biking though, but relatively thin-shelled, virtually padding free, cotton lined scull-cap or half-helmet affairs. Later, upon the arrival of the full-face item around the mid 1970s, these older helmets became known as open-face lids (lid was and is an abbreviation of skid-lid, an 'in' term for referring to all types of crash-helmet both then and now). Later still, these lids would be daubed with some form of hand-painted graphic which served several purposes. Firstly, it announced to other road users that the wearer was not your average motorcyclist; secondly it enabled fellow riders to recognise them - or their gang - by their unique design (many gang and club members shared similar designs); and thirdly, when fifty or sixty Bikers had gathered in a cafe and all the helmets were nonchalantly chucked wherever, the individual graphic would help the owner locate his or her head gear easier when it was time to leave. This individualising of an otherwise mundane protective item also acted as a precursor of what was to come as the 1960s dawned.

As stated though, helmets were not compulsory at that time, and not all elected to wear them. One major reason for this was that a skid-lid would flatten an elaborate Tony Curtis style quiff, or D.A. as it became known (D.A. standing for Ducks Arse, as even those sporting this hairstyle openly admitted that from the back that was exactly what it looked like). As a D.A. necessitated using much hair grease (Brylcreme being the most popular brand), the lining of the helmet would invariably end up looking and smelling disgusting. The D.A. was one legacy of the Teddy Boy carried over to this new mobile motorbike culture, as were the pointed toe winkle-picker boots which tended to be saved for the dance halls rather than the open road, as riding in them and safely using the foot operated gear-shift and rear brake mechanisms was a virtual impossibility. I know, I have tried!

By 1959, the D.A., the winkle-picker boot, and an unerring love of Rock & Roll were all that was left of the Teddy Boy in Britain. They no longer offered the mainstream look for all bad boys and wanna-be bad boys. They had become the cult accessories of the early Biker scene. Teenage fashion had moved on. Therefore, unlike the majority of the females they attracted, these were no longer teenagers but tearaways in their twenties. The very fabric of Western society was panic stricken by this, as it had become blindingly obvious that the alleged anti-social activity associated with adolescents since the beginning of that decade could no longer be contained by the age specific safety net of 'Teenager.' With this latest group's 'devil may care' preoccupation with achieving the magical 100 miles per hour at every possible opportunity, the general public saw these twenty-something motorcyclists as the scourge of the road and the press labelled them accordingly. The Ton-Up Boy had arrived. The question was, being so unpopular, where would he go?

The 1950s had seen the late night cafe and Milk Bar become the focal point for emerging trendy young things, but for the seemingly more mature Ton-Up Boys (and Girls) of Britain and America, the appeal of such establishments was limited. Instead, these mobile marauders chose the open road for their entertainment which (particularly in Britain) gave a new lease of life to an otherwise mundane and much maligned set of eateries: the transport cafe. These Greasy Spoons as they affectionately (and aptly) became known, lined the arterial trunk roads across the pre-motorway UK and USA.

By day these cafes were patronised by travelling sales people, tourists en-route from A to B, and lorry drivers. As night fell though, a select few became the domain of the Ton-Up Boys, who would race from one to another, congregate for a while with others of their kind for light-hearted barracking and camaraderie, then race back (or on). Sightseers and wanna-bees, too, would frequent these cafes (sometimes even dressed in leather and carrying a crash-helmet as they stepped from the bus or out of Dad's borrowed car), as these venues became the places to go to see motorcycles of all descriptions. On a good night, the forecourts of these hostelries would look more like the pits at a motorbike race meeting or an open-air racing motorcycle show than a car park. Ultimately, this resulted in the styles of bikes represented at these cafes being generically called 'Cafe Racers', a style and name which persists to this day.

Sometimes hundreds and hundreds of Cafe Racer

riding youths would descend on a single cafe on a given evening as a show of strength. Sometimes there would be a degree of inter-gang rivalry and trouble. On the whole though, high jinx and boisterous behaviour was all that the proprietor of any given cafe would have to endure, along with, of course, an increase in tea, egg and chip sales and Juke Box small coin trade. Ton-Up Kids were good for business, so many cafes started to cater for them specifically. Most of these are now sadly gone, but the names by which they were known, such as 'Johnson's Cafe' near Brands Hatch raceway in Kent, England, and the infamous 'Ace Cafe' in London (after which the aforementioned style of racing handlebars are allegedly named following their widespread use by the regulars there) in London, will always live on in motorcycling mythology. We will return to the Ace Cafe further on.

My coverage of 1950s Britain now ends but before we move through to the 1960s, we'll take a quick trip to America for a look at the establishment of the rights of passage and legacy of the lifestyle Biker.

chapter tWO:

the
Wild
one

Waitress: "What are you rebelling against?"
Johnny: "What have you got?"

From the film **The Wild One**,
produced by Stanley Kramer, 1953.

Pre-dating all of the aforementioned events in Britain, something truly important to Biker culture occurred in the US of A. Immediately after WWII, small groups of young American ex-military personnel began gravitating towards the motorcycle for free-spirited camaraderie and the open road, rather than the life of Joe Public. Normality was neither wanted nor relished and motorcycling helped them escape and be with others of their kind. They called their machines Cycles (an equally potent term to that of Bike) so as to differentiate themselves from the 'transport only' motorcyclist, but also to show that they were nothing to do with the seemingly straight-laced American Motor Cycle Association (the AMA).

This new breed of Cycle rider formed local gangs which at weekends would set off en-masse to roar around the outlying black-tops and towns of their cities looking for excitement. Highway and interstate motel coffee bars became the meeting places for these pioneers of early American Cycle culture, which in some areas resulted in them being called Coffee Bar Cowboys, while in others they became known as Cycle Tramps and/or Cycle Boys (note the evolutionary similarity to the British Ton-Up Boy and Cafe Racer of nearly a decade on). The use of these almost endearing titles was to be relatively short-lived as, within a matter of months, the Cyclists' purported malevolent behaviour would see them being referred to with far more sinister rhetoric.

Few of these 1940s American Cycle Gangs were interlinked or shared styles with groups outside their own areas. More often, these groups had quite different tastes, rules and influences. For instance, some gangs would only listen to (then) contemporary Jazz, others to early Country and Western and/or what is now known as Blue Grass, and some only to the remnant Big Band sounds of the day. The majority listened to all of the above though, and subsequently within a few years these musical influences would fuse together with elements of Gospel to create inaugural Rock & Roll: the music of the first truly interconnected Biking movement.

Early cycle gangs also tended to differ in their image, as some deliberately dressed in farmer-style bib and brace dungarees with chequered lumber jackets, while others favoured the full leather look - no prizes for guessing which guise endured. Certain Cycle groups were also fickle about which machines were acceptable. Some would only allow their members to ride machines manufactured by the Indian Motorycle Company, others only Harley-Davidsons, while a select few would only permit the imported British marques of Triumph and Vincent et al within their ranks. Despite this, the bigger gangs at that time embraced all motorcycle marques in those pre-Japanese import days for reasons of practicality and availability.

This was certainly the case for the group who brought the phenomenon of the angry young motorcycle rider to American prominence, via the press, following a series of exploits at Hollister, California, during the long hot summer of 1947.

Independence Day &
a Helluva 'Hollister' Hullabaloo!

The best part of ten years before the *Rock Around The Clock* incident at the Trocadero in England, the American media discovered Bike Gangs, as indeed did the small Californian town of Hollister. The town of Hollister is really quite small. I know, because on one long afternoon off, I rode there. By bike it is about half an hour from Santa Cruz in California, which in turn is about an hour from San Francisco's City Limits. It is situated within striking distance of the El Camino Real Mission (built in the 1700s) which in turn is famous for being located right on the San Andreas fault line. Hollister is more a place you go through than go to. But Hollister town is also unique in as much as it still harbours that Mid-West pioneer feel, due in part to its white-washed United States Post Office and 'Whiskey Creek' saloon. Why this inoffensive hamlet came to be besieged by Bikers en-masse one fateful day may always remain a mystery. The fact remains that it was, and as such the events in question will always be of quintessential cultural and historical importance for both the American and worldwide Biker alike.

On 4th July 1947 they rode into town attracted by an adjoining AMA sporting event. Exactly how many, or why, nobody really knows, but they did it none the less. Uncle Sam's perception of young men on motorcycles would never be the same again after these events unfolded. American mythology had found a latter-day replacement for the Cowboy gangs that plagued the frontier lands of Wyatt Earp and Doc Holliday. After 4th July, 1947, the American 'Out-Law' Biker (as they would become known) had arrived and was here to stay. Should he happen to roll into your town, be sure to lock up your daughter and hide Granny with your hooch. This extract from *Life Magazine* suggests why:

"On the 4th of July weekend, 4,000 members of a motorcycle club roared into Hollister, California, for a three-day convention. They quickly tired of ordinary motorcycle thrills and turned to more exciting stunts. Racing their bikes down the main street and through traffic lights, they rammed into restaurants and bars, breaking furniture and mirrors... Police arrested many for drunkenness and indecent exposure but could not restore order... after two days the cyclists left with a brazen explanation. 'We like to show off. It's just a lot of fun.' But Hollister's Police chief took a different view." (Life Magazine, 21st July 1947).

The influence of this report as it circulated melamine breakfast tables the length and breadth of North America that July was marked. It had a profound effect on American society as, following its publication, the Cycle Boy (or Cycle Bum as they became known), quickly graduated to being public enemy number one.

*　*　*

In conjunction with a wide array of politicians, law enforcement officials, scare-mongering journalists, moralists and religious figure-heads, the AMA - who were perceived as being thoroughly wholesome and as American as apple-pie - tried to shame this new breed of motorcyclist into extinction. Not only did they fail miserably, but because of the media exposure afforded them by those with whom they were in cahoots, they actually helped fan the flames that spread the allure of this seemingly abhorrent Cycle culture. They also unwittingly gave these Cycle Tramps their first interconnecting and unifying emblem, as explained below. From here on in, any attempt to banish these Cycle Boys to the history books would be like a broken pencil: pointless. God bless the AMA!

But what did the American Motorcycle Association get so wrong, and how could their actions have back-fired so dramatically? Perhaps most significantly, they underestimated the draw of this new culture and inadvertently helped the media offer these gangs huge public exposure. For example, in a much-publicised press release of the day, the AMA's Executive Secretary, a Mr Linton Kuchler referred repeatedly to the trouble-making Cycle Riders of the Hollister event as being of an 'Out-Law' ilk who only represented around one percent of American motorcyclists. Of course all this did was to guarantee instant 'Bad Boy' status for ANY young American who donned a leather jacket and straddled a Cycle. The escalation in the popularity of this image which followed such supposed negative publicity was unprecedented. From then on, nothing could stem the tide of Cycle disciples, and the American establishment knew it. And as for the one percent quip? Within days 1% badges were being crafted and worn with pride by those whom the comment was misguidedly designed to shame: the aforementioned emblem which is as potent today as indeed it was then.

Brando, Biker Bonding & Celluloid Cycling

During the 1940s and 1950s, America was dominated by movie culture (as it is today) for reasons far too complex to précis here. Suffice to say that during the middle of the 20th century, the United States of Hollywood already had a real influence on the American public (as highlighted by Dr Anthony Woodiwiss in his book, *Only In America*). Over and above any actual entertainment though, movie makers relished the moral outrage and panic they could create with a moving picture. So when an up-and-coming movie producer by the name of Stanley Kramer made the 1953 film *The Wild One*, starring a youthful Marlon Brando as Johnny, the leader of the Black Rebels Motorcycle Club, the public and the press sat up and took note. Directed by Laszlo Benedek and screen-written by John Paxton, this Stanley Kramer production draws its inspiration from a short story entitled 'The Cyclist Raid', written by Frank Rooney, which was published in an edition of *Harpers* magazine, post-Hollister and influenced by the same.

Filmed in black and white and in a sympathetic cinematic style to the westerns of the day, *The Wild One* also draws on the much-publicised events of the Hollister incident for the back-drop of its story-line. It also harbours a good old-fashioned love story, an attempt to demonstrate that good can triumph over evil, as well as the point that sinners can repent. I must admit though, as a kid watching this film for the first time, these latter considerations and plots were wasted on me. I only saw men being tough, lawless, afraid of nothing, and recklessly having fun aboard their bikes. I have not been alone in my seemingly blinkered and shallow interpretation of this film however, as (arguably) the majority of people who see it for the first time also come away holding only these facts, irrespective of whether this impresses, disgusts or frightens them.

Johnny (Brando) spoke slickly and rode a glossy black

35

British Triumph. He wore robust, snug-hugging denim jeans, bike boots, a well-fitting zip-up black leather bike jacket, and an almost paramilitary-style peaked cap tilted at a provocative slant. Johnny and his other 'Black Rebels' also had their club name emblazoned across the backs of their jackets in a design of studs. His adversary in the film was Chino, head of a rival motorcycle gang, played by Lee Marvin. Although some argue that the almost agricultural clothes worn by Chino probably bore more resemblance to how the Hollister hordes had really dressed, it was the aforementioned uniform of Johnny that influenced the wardrobes of the era's 'one percent' Bikers. This now classic piece of cinematography had given to the hitherto fragmented motorcycle movement of mid-20th century America, an identity and focus of national union. This image has since been adopted and subverted to some extent by gay culture, which has been drawn to its level of macho charisma, and as such is now unlikely to be seen in its unadulterated form on the back of a lifestyle Biker.

Brando Banned In Britain,
But Biker Bros Battle On!

Due to a draconian British censorship regime, *The Wild One* was not available for public consumption in the UK until some 15 years after its 1953 USA release, by which time it seemed dated and tame as the 'moment' had gone. This was brutally highlighted by a headline banner in the British-based *Daily Express* which read *'The Wild One Is Such A Mild One.'* Obviously, the writer who wrote this lacked the first basic skill of reviewing, which is to keep things in context.

Fortunately, images and photographic stills from *The Wild One* had landed in Britain years before the film via the press, which meant that by the mid-50s, Brit Bike Boys could share the imagery enjoyed by their Cycle-riding Stateside Brothers (Bros). This contributed greatly to the emerging UK Ton-Up Boy identity detailed earlier, and helped lay the foundations for the following generation of Rocking and Rolling riders who would take the 1960s by storm.

chapter three:

Born
to
be
Wild

The early 1960s saw the influence of Rock & Roll fade among the youth of the USA and UK, replaced instead by the growing transatlantic popularity of the British Beat-Bands that abounded (such as The Beatles and The Rolling Stones). The 'Swinging Sixties' as they became known, also saw significant social change. For within a few years the 1960s would play host to an expanding drug culture, and (due to the sexual emancipation of women brought about by the introduction of the contraceptive pill), a level of sexual freedom hitherto unheard of. The 1960s also witnessed the arrival of youth-styled tribal rivalry.

The magnitude of these rivalries was not fully understood by the public until a series of coastal clashes in 1964 brought them to prominence. But in order for the aforementioned altercations to take place, first, the rival factions had to be established. The tide of resurgent teenagers provided the foot soldiers for this, and their need to establish an identity the joint justification. To explain this phenomenon further, we need to backtrack a little.

As stated in the closing section of the last chapter, the Biker image of Brando from the film *The Wild One* was of significant importance to both American and British cult cycle riders alike. In the UK these influences helped the Ton-Up Boy emerge phoenix like from their fading embers of influence to reveal the rejuvenated Biker image now synonymous with the 1960s: the Rocker (so called because of their love of traditional Rock & Roll) resplendent in leathers adorned with potent painted logos, intricate designs of studs, chains, and badges. Also as mentioned previously, although Rockers did continue to recruit some new teenage followers at that time, the vast majority of their number were twenty-something by the 1960s, which irritated the up and coming teenagers of the day greatly. To them, Rockers were ageing relics of the past who should move over and stop hogging the limelight.

Fat chance!

The next generation of style conscious young Britons after the Teds looked to Europe for fashionable inspiration when the 1950s and 1960s met, and the 'Continental Look' came into vogue. French and Italian clothes were adopted and adapted until they offered the perfect look for those with a thirst for both change and individuality. The then thriving Coffee Bar scene became the forum via which these new dress codes spread. To flaunt their fashions at the right cafes though, these teenagers needed to be mobile. Cars were too expensive and motorcycles perceived as too dirty. But the Italian motor-scooters of the period offered the perfect solution. They were cheap to run and added to the all important continental image. The scooters they rode had to meet certain cultural criteria to count though. They had to be either the marques of Lambretta or Vespa, and had to be 125cc or above (although 175cc and up were best). Anything short of this seriously diminished the rider's street-credible scooter credentials.

Initially calling themselves 'Individualists' or 'Stylists', these youngsters predilection for all things modern resulted in them being called 'Modernists', which was later abbreviated to 'Mods'. Over the next few years the Mod movement went from strength to strength in the UK, as it found a new breeding ground in the youth of the working classes. The scooter, too, enjoyed increased cultural status during this period, and soon became an all important icon of the Mod movement. To differentiate their machines from the 'transport only' scooter riders of the day, most Mods personalised their machines through the addition of chromed accessories, chromed and polished body panelling, and/or the fitting of an array of extra mirrors and spot lights to taste.

Scooter riding also indirectly provided the general public with the most identifiable item of Modernist dress, the Parka. Initially only available from army surplus stores, these American ex-military coats soon found their way into the fashionable boutiques of

Swinging London and beyond. The adoption by the Mods of this khaki cover-all was born out of practicality in exactly the same way as was the adoption of the leather jacket by the motorcycling Teds and Ton-Up Boys of the 1950s: protection from the elements while riding a two-wheeled motorised machine.

Mods & Rockers:
"We'll Fight Them On The Beaches"

Despite each adhering to two-wheeled transport, the Mods and Rockers hated each other with a passion. The Mods thought Rockers and their bikes were dirty, unkempt and outmoded, whereas the Rockers thought the Mods effeminate and their scooters a travesty. To expand on this and explain what happened next, I give you another passage from *Scooter Boys*.

"Both the Mods and Rockers now had a clearly defined and very different identity and ideology. There was more than just a generation gap separating them. They were vehemently opposed to one another, and it showed. The Mods would in time win the press propaganda war, but it would be the Rockers who would stand the test of time through rejuvenation and persistence.

Because of their cultural differences, the Mods and Rockers seldom came into contact with each other. This was more by luck than judgement, as to pursue their chosen lifestyles necessitated visiting different venues. But when a confrontation did occur, all and sundry sat up and took notice.

The Great British working class tradition of migrating to coastal resorts over Bank Holiday weekends was not wasted on the Mods and Rockers who would saddle up their steeds - along with hundreds of their contemporaries - and set off for their chosen coastal port of call. It was a foregone conclusion that, before long, both factions' destination would eventually prove to be one and the same." (Scooter Boys *by Gareth Brown, 6th edition. Independent Music Press 2001. First published 1989).*

After the British Bank Holiday weekend of March 30th 1964, the front page lead story of *The Daily Mail* newspaper reported on events which allegedly happened at the Essex coastal resort of Clacton:

"The Wild Ones invaded a seaside town yesterday, one thousand fighting, drinking, roaring, rampaging teenagers on scooters and motorcycles. By last night, after a day of riots and battles with police, ninety seven of them had been arrested."

... And on May 19th 1964 following the Whitsun weekend, the lead story in *The Daily Sketch* further fuelled the nation's moral panic by reporting:

"Stabbing, stoning, deck-chair battles. The Wild Ones of Whitsun went even wilder yesterday with two beach stabbings, attacks on police and violent clashes between Mods and Rockers. Holiday-makers cowered as the rampaging spread from Margate in Kent to other south coast resorts - especially Brighton."

By 1965 however, the British press had begun to relegate reports of Mod and Rocker rivalry to that of a filler item, and by 1966 their coverage had disappeared completely. Mods and Rockers it appeared, had lost both their newsworthiness and appeal. Mod was dead (for now) as a mainstream movement and the Rocker's ranks were waning. This was due in part to the nature of fashion coupled with the inevitable desire of each generation to establish an identity of its own. It was time for change.

Times They Are A-Changin'

By the middle of 1967, the so-called 'summer of love', everything had changed. Fashion had started a natural metamorphosis towards the pending Californian Hippy craze and, where they existed (predominantly the UK), Mods traded in their parkas for either a Hippy-style caftan coat, or a Crombie (explained further on), or left the arena of youthful endeavour altogether. This 'Flower Power' period as it became known, also gave the world a number of musical anthems and standards which have most admirably stood the test of time: the most poignant (and my favourite) of which are now listed.

'California Dreaming' by The Mamas & The Pappas.
'San Francisco (wear some flowers in your hair)'
by Scott McKenzie.
'Sunshine Of Your Love' by Cream.
'Summer In The City' by the Lovin' Spoonful.
'She'd Rather Be With Me' by The Turtles.

In 1969 American cinematography reflected the changes that 'Hippiedom' and the possibility of being drafted to fight in Vietnam was having on their home-grown male Bikers, and offered for consumption a feature film which rapidly became equally as potent as Brando's *The Wild One* had done fifteen years earlier. This was a new movie for a new generation of cycle riders, and a movie which within weeks traversed the globe giving the youth of the world their next - and enduring - time specific motorcycling identity. The film was *Easy Rider*. Written by Peter Fonda and Dennis Hopper (the film's two leading actors) along with Terry Southern, and filmed under the executive production of Bert Schneider and photographic directorship of Laszlo Kovacs, this movie was destined to have a sizeable impact.

Filmed against the philosophical idiom of the era of

tune in, turn on and drop out, *Easy Rider* set souls on fire and provoked - predictably - a new wave of moral panic as many young petrol-heads started to emulate the Biker image portrayed by this piece of cinema. Unlike *The Wild One* though, this movie only features two cycle-riding individuals: Wyatt (Peter Fonda) and Billy (Dennis Hopper). The *Easy Rider* story shares the nomadic genre of *The Wild One* though, whereby after an initial illicit drug trafficking transaction, focusses around the allure and atmosphere of the forthcoming 'Mardi Gras' party in New Orleans and the camaraderie, people and experiences encountered by Hopper and Fonda en-route across America.

Ending with two Hill-Billies from an amazingly small gene pool expressing their disapproval of Wyatt and Billy's lifestyle with the aid of a twelve gauge amidst cries of 'get your hair cut', *Easy Rider* was - and is - far more than just another bike or road movie. For not only did this film highlight an attitude towards Bikers from some quarters of which to be wary, it gave many of the world's Bikers a revitalised direction with which to embrace the forthcoming 1970s. It also signalled an exciting catalyst of change in cycle-customising circles: the chopper, as ridden by the two central characters of Wyatt and Billy.

Chopper Cycles: Style & Sedition

The original concept of the chopper cycle is firmly fixed in American biking history. The ethos behind the custom chopper has also inspired an array of global customising styles since the 1960s which are represented to this day through the genius of many motorcycle 'customizing' craftsmen and visionaries such as Arlen Ness, whose mobile masterpieces rank among some of the most inspiring and aesthetically pleasing machines imaginable. The US-based origins of the chopper owe much to the British bike stables of Triumph, BSA and Norton, and the British-led Cafe Racer look however, as without the existence of these styles and influences, the motorcycle modification bug which bit 1950s and 1960s America - and ultimately lead to the design brief for the classic chopper - may never have materialised.

Of the American servicemen who had been to Europe during World War II, many had an interest in motorcycles, and as such, were delighted at what they discovered there: British bikes. Once back at home with Uncle Sam, many of these men favoured the lightweight, streamlined sports machines they had seen in the UK in preference to their own home-grown steeds, such as Indian and Harley-Davidson which they felt were too cumbersome. This thirst was both fuelled and quenched by British motorcycle imports to the USA and the Cafe Racer trend. This in turn created an increase in demand for lightweight sports-bikes (as did Marlon Brando astride a Triumph in the film *The Wild One*) which in turn created a greater demand for British bikes Stateside at a time when the British motorcycle industry really did rule the two-wheeled world.

Harley-Davidson counteracted this demand for streamlined sports machines slightly by introducing their own lightweight bike (although still a V-twin) in 1952 which they called the K. Also known as the Sportster, it wasn't until H-D introduced the significantly improved XL version in 1957 that they really started to regain ground in this sector of the 'new' bike market. By then, an array of other lightweight American motorcycles had also started to appear alongside their British counterparts in the USA, courtesy of customization. With this generation of bikes, predominantly from the marques of Harley-Davidson and/or Indian, in essence, it was their manufacturer's names and engines alone which linked them to the factories from which they had once hailed. Almost universally their outward appearances had been altered in many instances to a point beyond formal recognition and specification.

Often unable to afford or justify a streamlined new British import, many American motorcyclists acquired affordable second-hand examples of their home-grown big and bulky bikes, and set about reworking them by removing much of the heavy fendering they sported and, in all but 'total loss' models, replacing the twin tanks with single, slimmer, sportier examples which boasted an array of eye-catching liveries. Some of these custom motorcycle pioneers even modified or made alternative frames with exaggerated front forks to enhance the stripped look in which to mount their engines. This started an on-going organic process which ultimately led to the hybrid blueprint of the archetypal classic chopper now synonymous with mid-1960s America and *Easy Rider*.

Featuring overly extended forks, altered rake yokes, hard-tails, high-rise bars, ornate painted peanut gas tanks and chromed hand-crafted sissy bars (pillion back rests), the chopper cycles ridden by both Hopper and Fonda in *Easy Rider* set the standards which all other choppers would have to follow. In America, these machines were - and are - predominantly powered by V-Twin Harley motors. In the UK British engines provided the majority of the power-plants during the 1960s and 1970s when the chopper craze arrived there, although by the 1980s examples of Japanese technology could be found propelling such machines everywhere but in the USA. Before exploring this 1980s oriental influence further however, let us return to the period immediately post-*Easy Rider*, say goodbye to the Swinging Sixties, and embrace fully the arrival of the Savage Seventies.

chapter fOur:

the

saVage

Seventies

By the 1970s, the international Biker movement had started to spread beyond America and Britain. In many countries such as Germany, Austria, the Benelux countries, Scandinavia, Australia and New Zealand (to name but a few), their numbers reached what the authorities perceived as being of epidemic proportions. The unified image perpetuated alongside the motorcycle at that time (which ideally had to be a chopper) was heavily influenced by *Easy Rider*, although it had been amalgamated with a cocktail of other influences including remnants of Brando's *The Wild One* and elements of Hippy fashion. Within a few years, this universal Biker image was unmistakable across the globe, with only nominal national subtleties setting each country apart. A new name started to be used by the press of the day to describe this new breed of Biker – 'The Greaser' had been officially categorised and labelled.

Hair was worn long by these Greasers, and mutton chop sideburns and later full beards grown. Jeans were unavoidably oil-stained, flared and by Levi, and leather jackets covered with similarly oil splattered cut-offs. A cut-off or set of 'colours' (the term used to describe a given motorcycle club's particular motif and name) as they are also known, is basically a denim jacket (again preferably by Levi) with the sleeves removed, which is worn over the top of a leather jacket to display the badges and identifying graphics of their group. Previously, these would have been fixed directly to the leather item itself. However, the separation of the cut-off from the leather jacket allowed a degree of anonymity when needed, while still maintaining the protection of the leather when riding. Then, at an appropriate time and place, the cut-off could be easily returned to its more overt location on top of the leather. By the 1980s, leather cut-offs were being manufactured by tanners sympathetic to Biker life. These were more durable than their denim counterparts, and (arguably) looked a whole lot better; nonetheless examples of their denim predecessor still prevail in some quarters to this day, and probably always will.

Other aspects of the Biker culture also evolved in the 1970s. Helmets - where worn and where possible - were ex-German army, and sometimes chromed and polished, but usually as standard complete with original insignias. German Iron Crosses (original and/or reproduction) were also used to adorn many cut-offs in America and Britain, as in the words of a friend of mine at that time "Our Dads fought the Germans in the War. What better way is there to piss them off than wear the medals of their enemy?" These pieces of regalia were not adopted by all Biking countries (then or now) though, for blatantly obvious reasons.

The philosophy of wearing the Iron Cross is explained further by the following transcript from an interview with a Biker called Tony, billed as a rebel rocker, from a 1969 BBC television documentary entitled *A Year In The Life*. The transcript is taken from Tony's response to being asked about his anti-social and malevolent behaviour, and brings firmly into question the mythology that the late 1960s and early 1970s were a time of youthful Hippy-inspired peace and tranquillity.

"What it is, is we are living in their world and we don't like it. We want to change it and the only way we can change it is by rearing up... We can't change it by talk or anything because they won't listen. They say we are not old enough or sensible enough so what you've got to do is make them feel really sick with you..."

*   *   *

The predominance of the supposed harmonious Hippy folklore was at stark odds to the actual experiences of many youths such as Tony. Admittedly, many Hippy types did demonstrate against such things as the atomic bomb and the Vietnam War (while in many instances openly extolling the virtues of hallucinogens), and furthermore the commercial aspect of Flower Power did inspire open-air music events such as the Woodstock concert in America and Isle of Wight weekend in England. Culturally, however, things were not all peace and harmony. Elsewhere, equally large numbers of youths were being influenced by an entirely different sequence of events. However, hippies and their endeavours were deemed more newsworthy, which ultimately has resulted in their sentiments, actions, and spheres of influence being disproportionately represented by an array of post-1970 journalists. In many instances, these journalists have thus created an imbalanced picture of how things really were in the 1970s, by portraying the era in question through their own value-laden and rose-tinted spectacles.

Truth is, for many members of the younger generation, beneath the veneer of purported peace and love, the late 1960s and early 1970s were violent, very violent, especially in Britain (exacerbated by the growing scourge of soccer hooliganism). The following extract from a report in *The Daily Mail* newspaper in September 1969 concerning the Isle of Wight music festival highlights this paradox:

"While 150,000 young fans were peaceably communing with Mr Bob Dylan on the Isle of Wight, eighty miles away in North London a gang of youths were doing their best to kick in the face of a thirteen-year-old boy. The youths were Skinheads who, in contrast to the Hippy's vague and shaggy line of gentle coexistence, preach an alarming new doctrine of destruction."

* * *

Hippies were predominantly the offspring of the middle classes. Skinheads were the next big British street level working class cult after Mod, and a natural progression of the Modernist's smart image, which the Skinheads perverted and parodied through G.I.-style cropped hair, the introduction of highly polished working man's boots (first from a company called Tuff and later Dr Martens) and city gents Crombie overcoats. In many instances, initially, these early Skinheads also used Italian motor-scooters, although in an anti-statement of Mod they not only removed all the frivolous bolt-on chrome accessories associated with Mod scooters, but took the strip-down look yet further by removing and/or cutting down parts of the body panelling until said machines looked almost skeletal (this look was more effective on the tubular spine constructed Lambretta than on the chubby pressed-framed Vespa).

You haven't got to be an Einstein here then to realise that with Skinheads being the new Scooter Boys of the day, and Greasers the latest incarnation of the Biker, troubles reminiscent of the Mod and Rocker beach battles of 1964 were not only likely, but inevitable. The seafront at Southend-on-Sea, Essex, England, and later Margate, Kent, provided the venues for many such reported altercations over a succession of Bank Holiday weekends from 1969 through to 1971. By 1972, such incidents started to be reported less and less and by 1973, as the mainstream Skinhead movement petered away, such reports ceased. Globally, however, Greaser-associated violence persisted in the press throughout the 1970s. Many Flower-Power followers were politicised at that time, with strong allegiances to the far left. Some even erred towards the West's biggest taboo: communism. These deluded themselves that the revolution was just around the corner, and some that the international Biker fraternity was their Praetorian guard, their vanguard against suppression, and their own front line troops who would rise up and fight for them on command when the glorious day arrived. Ha ha! Obviously they had experimented a little too often with the hallucinogenic drugs that they - and others of their kidney - were purportedly trying to legalise...

Bikers were and are fiercely loyal to a cause - their cause. They would do almost anything to protect and defend it. But rise up and fight for a bunch of Hippies? Think again, mystic men, think again. True, many Bikers were political at that time, but their views spread from those sympathetic with the left, right through to those who can be argued to have attached items of Nazi memorabilia to their cut-offs for reasons other than shock value. But in the main, these politics were left outside the theatre of biking, as to Bikers, the internal politics of their given calling were - and are - often more important than those outside. Coupled with the fact that most of these political agitators were viewed by Bikers as pigeon-chested wimps with whom they wanted nothing to do, if ever said activists over-stepped the mark, they ran the risk of being reminded of such via a good old-fashioned Biker-style SLAP!

Many Greasers did fight for groups in the 1970s though, but not in preparation for any pending revolution. They fought against those who threatened or challenged their authority (like the Mods and Skinheads in England) or their territory, which in certain areas of the world meant fighting others of their kind.

From its earliest days, cycle culture has been dominated by gang loyalties and rivalries, as depicted in *The Wild One*. By the 1990s this facet of Biker-life had escalated into a complex hierarchical club scene complete with aligned actions and etiquette. These seemingly feudal systems are far from draconian though. But before the well-evolved 1990s status quo was achieved, we had the 1980s, and before that, the subject of discussion here: the 'savage Seventies', which can best be expressed by the following short story.

The year was 1972. For one reason or another I was in Essex, England. It was a hot sticky June evening, and I had been attracted to an event in the village of Danbury, about seven miles out from the county town of Chelmsford. Normally this was a quiet well-to-do little hamlet, but on this occasion, it was to be the staging point for a Greaser upon Greaser conflict. In what must have been the centre of the village was a large hall with a shingle car park and an adjoining field of some considerable size. Traditional 1950s style Rock & Roll was blurting out from the hall as I arrived amidst the pink hue of dusk, courtesy of a most passable local band. In the car park were what seemed like hundreds of British motorbikes of all shapes, sizes and styles. These were parked in two distinctly different and demarked zones.

The hall and car park were virtually void of revellers though, as the vast majority of people appeared to be congregating in the field. A large group of spectators were gathered at the car park end, while in the middle stood what seemed like two massive groups of motorcyclists. These groups had removed their leather jackets, but replaced their cut-offs over an assortment of T-shirt and vest tops, and some seemed to be holding bike chains or spanners. On the backs of one set of cut-offs were written the words 'Billericay Bastards', and on the others 'Danbury Tigers'. This was the Tiger's patch, but the 'Billericay Bastards' believed themselves to be top dogs in Essex at that time, and were here to prove it. There then followed some shouting and gesturing before BOSH, it all went off!

The two gangs moved in on each other like so many medieval warriors. Girls in the spectator sector screamed, Bikers in the thick of it screamed, and claret ran freely as metal implement after metal implement collided purposefully with flesh and bone. After what seemed like only a couple of seconds the two groups separated, with several of their number clutching bloody heads. From where I stood there had been no clear victor, although as both teams hastily collected their gear, mounted their machines, and sped away in opposite directions ahead of the arrival of the Police (whose bells were now clearly audible), each proclaimed they had spanked the other side's arse.

This had been a good old-fashioned turf war between two back patch clubs, neither of which made it past the 1970s.[3] Before we move to the next chapter though, first, a quick vox-pop tour of the music which got the Greasers of the 1970s rocking.

Footnote 3
A term explained in the following chapter under the section headed Back Patches & Front Patches: MCs & MCCs.

Long Live Rock

Ignoring Glam Rock and Punk (which I am the first to admit were both great forms of music for different reasons), the 1970s were musically extremely important in Biker terms. The 70s music scene smashed an array of barriers and provided lifestyle motorcyclists everywhere with a plethora of new sounds. The days of cult cyclists only being able to publicly like the 1950s style sounds of Rock & Roll were over. Greasers had it good. Their image was new and developing, and the restrictions governing what they should or should not listen to were open to 'what's new'? And what was new was Rock, and a particularly potent derivative therein called Heavy Metal. This latter sound was angry, aggressive, loud and dynamic. Rock symbolised an attitude, but Heavy Metal drove parents wild with rage. Rock and Heavy Metal were not purely the domain of the biking fraternity however, as they turned kids on from all walks of life.

Many Rock and Metal performers at that time dressed in a pastiche of the Greaser look though, and some openly extolled the virtue of the motorcycle. This influenced more teenagers to embrace motorcycle ownership than previously may have been tempted, thus swelling the Biker's ranks yet further. Rock and Heavy Metal can be argued to have been the next natural stage in guitar sound, an amalgamated hybrid of what had been considered raucous in the 60s, combined with the bass-heavy sounds of artists like Hendrix. As I'm not a popular music historian however, and as this isn't a book about music, we'll leave the development of Rock and Heavy Metal here for those interested to research it elsewhere (see Bibliography). Before leaving the sounds of the seventies behind completely and moving to the 1980s though, and in time honoured tradition, I give you three Heavy Metal/Rock standards which, for me, sum up the essence of the 1970s Greaser scene perfectly.

'Ace Of Spades' by Motorhead.
'Paranoid' by Black Sabbath.
'Born To Be Wild' by Steppenwolf.

chapter fiVe:

the
Enlightenment

As the 1970s rolled on, and 'pure' Punk Rock came and went - leaving in its wake a profusion of commercialised bland offerings purportedly of the same ilk - the Biker movement underwent yet further changes. In time these would incorporate elements of Punk in certain sectors, but most importantly, another name change. Names like Greaser and Rocker were assigned to the history books as, at last, Bikers became known right across the board as just that, Bikers, thanks to a seemingly enlightened press and public awareness. The now universally acknowledged Biker movement went from strength to strength as it embraced the turn of the decade amidst an array of youth culture revivals. These revivals saw the resurgence of Mod, Skinhead, Teddy Boys, traditional Rockers and Head-Bangers. The latter of these was the 70s term for followers of Heavy Metal, whose image incorporated aspects of Glam Rock and Greaser: the name derived from the style of dancing which accompanied Metal music. Some believe these revivals were spawned by the void left among the young after the purification effect of Punk on the popular music scene. Such tribal groups started in Britain and soon spread, as did the inevitable inter-tribal altercations. The following quote from a police officer in Brighton, England, as published in the national British press over the August Bank Holiday weekend of 1981, admirably highlights this resurgence of tension.

"We've got the lot this weekend, Skinheads, Mods, Rockers, Punks, Teddy Boys, Head-Bangers, we've got the lot. Keeping them apart is not going to be easy... And if we can't? Well, God help the residents of Brighton."

* * *

Although some traditional Mod vs Rocker, and Skinhead vs Greaser/Head-Banger violence did erupt, the most vicious and on-going feuds at that time were those of Punks vs Teds, and Mods vs Skins. These left the authorities in a confused whirl, although at street level, they were not only understandable but fully justifiable. Punk and Ted represented the first and (then) last press propaganda images of youth, and as such were obliged to loathe each other. The actual relationship between Mods and Skins was akin to that of big and baby brother, culturally, so these groups were too close for comfort and conflict was also inevitable. By the mid-80s, the Punk image had entered the realms of nostalgia and as such lost the vigour of violence.

As Punk thus joined the Teddy Boy as a movement populated in the main by ageing devotees, hostilities between these two ceased. Mods and Skins, meanwhile, underwent an on-going transition. Some moved on from these chosen revivalist lifestyles to other things or left youth culture behind completely, while some joined the nostalgic ranks of Teds and Punks by perpetuating the purest forms of Modernism and Skinhead. Most found solace, guidance and camaraderie by morphing into the cult of the Scooter Boy or Scooterist, where - due to the increasing tolerance and age of their number - a state of relative mutual understanding developed between them and Bikers, albeit underlined by 'close to the knuckle' derision and piss-taking.

The Enigmatic Eighties

Other than the motorcycle and aligned clubs (which will be returned to later), the two things that have acted as the social glue of the international Biker scene since the 1980s can be argued to be the periodicals the movement has spawned, and the events which they report. These periodicals come in the form of magazines such as *Easy Riders* (predominantly a US title although available the world over), and *Back Street Heroes*, which was - and is - an influential force in Europe. Other titles that have hit the limelight since the 1970s are *Custom Cycle*, *Heavy Duty*, *Street Fighters* and *Outlaw Biker* (to name but a few). In each case, these periodicals/magazines have adopted a similar format. Each is around A4 size with scores of glossy photographs of customised motorcycles and technical reports; each usually has at least one raunchy 'Bird on a Bike' shot (usually on the cover); and each carries articles and tuning tips on how to hot up your Hog (an affectionate term for Harley-Davidsons) or other marques. Each also carries reports about biking events.

These events are prolific and varied, although all involve amassing with hundreds or thousands of fellow Bikers at a specific time in a specific location for an initial specific reason (drag and/or race meets, custom shows, or club parties). Most involve camping, drinking, live music, trade stalls (to varying degrees) and generally having a good time. During the 1980s, the most noted (and largest) of these were the annual events at Sturgis and Daytona in the USA (both of which are still very well-attended to this day), the Bull-Dog Bash drag meet held in Warwickshire, England, as well as the Kent Custom Bike Show, Kent, England. Sadly, the KCBS no longer takes place, but in order to mark its importance in British Biker culture, and in order to give those of you who have never attended such an event a feel for them, I give you a transcript of a report from an edition of *Heavy Duty* magazine (which itself is now no longer available) reproduced with the kind permission of both the scribe responsible and one of the magazine's past publishers.

The Kent Custom Bike Show
(Angel Park, Dymchurch, Kent, July 12th, 13th & 14th 1991).

It was fast approaching mid-July and the annual Kent Custom Bike Show. Weeks of relentless rain had finally given way to the more traditional sunshine associated with the show weekend, and right across the continent members of the biking fraternity were savouring their anticipation in preparation for the off. For most show-goers, the mass migration towards the Kent coast, and Dymchurch in particular, started with avengeance on the Friday morning, although for many, the Mecca on the marsh would not be reached until later that evening.

With the rest of the motley crew who masquerade as the 'Heavy Duty' team already on site, I set off for Angel Park on Friday with my recently revamped Harley FXR closely resembling a Klondike prospector's pack horse. After circumnavigating the Medway towns, I soon found myself Ashford bound on the A20. There was then no mistaking what weekend this was, for at every turn of the road, at every junction, in every service station and outside almost every cafe and pub along my route were hundreds upon hundreds of bikes in every guise imaginable.

The sun was working hard to brighten the journey (although this wouldn't last) and make sure that everyone's weekend started off on the right note as Ashford was left behind and England's rural garden unravelled in front. The prolific procession of never-ending motorcycles weaved across the landscape like so many guided missiles, each destined to reach its target with Schwarzkopf-style pin point accuracy thanks to the 'KCBS this way' signs which lined the last ten or so miles to the show ground.

Imagine if you can, a packet of frozen peas being poured through a funnel. Now replace your mental peas with bikes and riders, and assume the show's private approach road to be the funnel's wider end, because that is exactly how it was. A brace of bobbies were doing their level best to keep the traffic flowing on the public highway, while a flurry of feverish activity at the gate ensured tickets were purchased and/or checked as quickly as possible in order to keep the unexpectedly high volume of early arrivals moving. It was then that I realised attendance at this year's show stood a good chance of reaching an all time high.

The recently re-gravelled rough road leading to the show ground's bowels was standing up particularly well to the sheer volume of vehicles passing over it, but unfortunately that was to change as the days rolled on. To the right of the gate was the official Kent Custom Bike Show control centre, private Hells Angels' enclosure and marshal's quarters, while in front were rapidly filling camping fields. To the left was the main stage and entertainment centre including the beer tent and caterers, while lining the field's perimeters were the trader's market stalls. With my tent erect and the compulsory 'hellos' taken care of, I went for a quick wander before searching out a six-pack and proclaiming that 'The Weekend Starts Here.'

Two things really struck me as I mooched about the show site. Firstly, and for me most pleasing, was the variety of international number plates I clocked along with their owners. Within the first fifteen minutes I encountered sizable contingents from Germany, Belgium, France, Holland, Austria, Sweden, and even a small group from Spain. The second thing which struck me was just how many of the bikes present were Harley-Davidsons. The ratio seemed quite literally to be (at least) one in ten. This situation really was a far cry from my first KCBS back in '85, when Harleys seemed so rare that wherever one was parked an adoring crowd was sure to gather. This year you could hardly take two steps without a gleaming example of the great American freedom machine springing into site.

The good weather prevailed into the early evening and beyond when Dell Steven's disco bowed out to the live entertainers

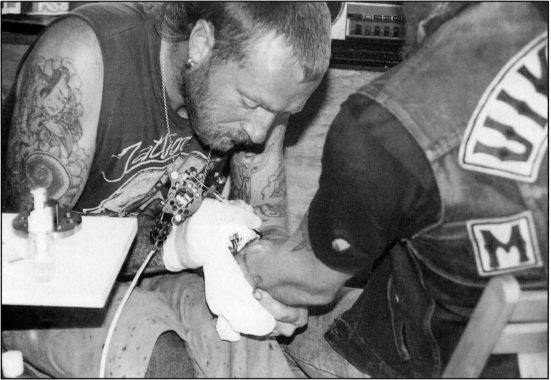

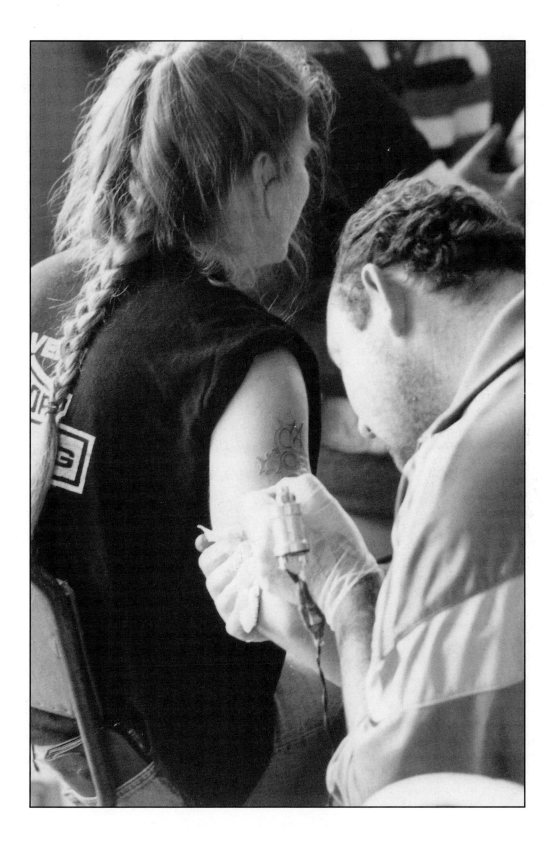

around 6pm. The evening's line-up included the Tom Palmer Band and the Hamsters, both of whom executed truly tremendous sets and went down well with the audience packed in front of the stage. Exhausted yet exhilarated by the overwhelming air of electrical excitement still lingering after the stage shut down at midnight, I went in search of food, the available diversity of which was astonishing. Apart from the obligatory burgers, hot dogs and chips, there were potato stalls, pancake stalls, vegetarian stalls, pizza stalls, and a Chinese. What is more, and as directed by the organisers, most of the food wrappings were bio-degradable. Fun, frolics and ecology all in the same weekend? Whatever next?

Then, clutching half a fried chicken, I took up position beside the main gate and watched in disbelief at the steady stream of bikes still bouncing up the rough road out of the night. The onslaught of new arrivals continued almost uninterrupted for the entire hour I sat there, and well into Saturday afternoon. I then tracked down a couple of drinking partners and headed off to the all night beer tent and the host of live bands playing there. The whole of the beer tent was packed. Not packed like the throbbing mass in front of the stage earlier, but packed in as much as all the stools, benches and tables were occupied. A mixture of live bands and DJs punctuated what was left of the night, along with copious pots of ale. People sat and talked, sang, or simply jumped about. One way or the other, all present were ensuring that they had a good time.

Saturday July 13th
Feeling particularly tender, this day started all too soon after the previous night had ended. However, unperturbed, I went about my business. Then the 13th struck! It was about 10am when the rain actually began although throughout the small hours the odd shower had damped the ground in preparation. But 10am stood out as the watershed, quite literally, for it was then that the sky grew grey and the heavens really opened. Falling with varying degrees of intensity, it rained relentlessly well into the evening, but did little to dampen anyone's enjoyment (although all present could have done with a cure for trench foot by the Sunday).

Initially, the twenty or so thousand people present either crammed themselves into the trade marquees and beer tents for cover, or sheltered in their own canvass dwellings thinking that the rain would soon pass. Within a couple of huddled hours though, most donned their 'Sod it, what's a little rain?' heads, and continued about their business. However, it was the enclosed attractions like the wall of death, the beer tent, and the female mud wrestling marquee which really reaped the benefits of this sudden bout of inclement weather, and not the attractions out in the open.

As morning rolled into afternoon and afternoon into evening, conditions underfoot became, quite frankly, appalling. Tractor loads of straw were hurriedly brought onto site and liberally strewn over the remnants of the main thoroughfares but to no avail. Because of the entirely undaunted manner in which the revellers were doing what they came to do, the straw very quickly disappeared into the mud and the main routes around Angel Park returned to goo. The evening entertainment kicked off with the obligatory wet T-shirt competition. Taking slightly more care than usual due to the slippery slosh separating teetering toes from terra firma, the concentration of the crowd in front of the stage intensified in more ways than one. Bands performing this evening included the Gutter Brothers and R Cajun & The Zydeco Bros (among others) topped off by Debbie Harry (Blondie). What an excellent night this was!

Sunday July 14th
The rain had gone but its after-effects hadn't. The blue skies and sunshine which greeted the day had more than just a little job on their hands drying out this particular section of Kent. The mass motorcycle exodus was already well underway by 9am, and I joined it. Have you ever seen the film The Pride and the Passion? *You know the one where Frank Sinatra leads a band of Spanish freedom fighters against the French? Well, do you remember the scene where they had to drag their great big cannon through a muddy river? That is exactly what it was like trying to get my Harley out of Angel Park that day. I wasn't alone though, as*

all around me were thousands of similarly suffering folk. Wheels were locking with lumps of soggy clay or simply spinning hopelessly, riders were being suddenly separated from their steeds, some bikes were so entrenched and immovable that their owners just gave up and sat there, and the traffic on the main road had to be periodically stopped so that the mud from departing vehicles could be scraped clear. But was it all worth it? Will I be back next year? You better believe it." (Heavy Duty *magazine, October1991*).

Back Patches & Front Patches:
MCs & MCCs

The Kent Custom Bike Show was organised annually for fifteen years by the Kent Chapter of the Hells Angels (HA) Motorcycle Club (MC), and towards the end of its run was held on land that the HA actually owned (Angel Park). This event always provided maximum Biker entertainment and fun, and on six occasions when I was in the UK at the right time I attended. I loved it, as each time I went, the weekend seemed to run like clock-work. What else would you expect from such a well-run and disciplined club? The HA have copyright on their logos and insignias, and a superior heritage to most which spans back to the Hollister debacle and a group of ex-WWII US Air Force bomber operatives turned Bikers who had referred to themselves during their war-time sorties as 'Hells Angels'. The HA are a select MC which can only be joined by initial invitation followed by an arduous period of 'prospecting'. This can span many years. Once elevated from prospect member to fully-fledged Angel though, an individual can wear the red and white top and bottom rocker decals and Deaths Head emblem (colours) of the HAMC on their cut-offs. The Hells Angels are a back patch club, and arguably the original and most elite. In the eyes of many of the international community however, this also makes them the archetypical outlaw motorcyclists. Since the 1950s, this has resulted in the most infuriating of adopted generic terms, wherein any motorcyclist deemed a nuisance is labelled a Hells Angel by the untutored press and public, irrespective of any earned or un-earned HA credentials the motorcyclist(s) in question may or may not have.

Other examples of back patch clubs include the Vietnam Vets, the Bandidos, the Chosen Few, Satan's Slaves and the Outlaws, to list but a few. All back patch clubs appear to operate along similar lines to one another, and most seem to only operate within their own geographical spheres of influence as, in the main, the turf wars of the 1970s (as highlighted by the anecdote of the last chapter) appear to be a thing of the past. This status quo is good. All MCs argue that they are the best though, which on occasion inevitably ends in altercation, as all back patch clubs are fiercely loyal to their colours and have a propensity for defending their club's honour. Back patch clubs use the initials MC (Motor Cycle Club) alongside their names and logos as opposed to the initials MCC (Motorcycle Club), as the latter communicates via the extra C that its wearer is not involved or interested in outlaw/gang-land Biking, and as such wishes to be left out of any lifestyle Biker power wrangles that may materialise. MCC members enthuse about motorcycles with others of their kind in an unthreatening way while still being able enjoy the camaraderie of club membership.

Often, these MCCs don't even sport a club graphic on their cut-offs so as to avoid any unlikely misinterpretation of their chosen status, and opt instead for a simple front patch above the left pocket which simply displays their club name and/or the aforementioned letters MCC. These have become known as front patch clubs, and can be found the world over alongside many branches of single make owners clubs such as the Harley Owners Group (HOG), whose number these days are predominantly made up of born again forty-something weekend Bikers with assurances and family health plans. The vast majority of Bikers are still unaffiliated free spirits however, whose approach to life has undeniably helped perpetuate the allure of cult motorcycling. In turn, the complexities of the late 20th and now 21st century club infrastructures as detailed can be argued to have maintained peace by keeping angry young men in check. One mild rivalry will continually rear its head among biking circles, although the end results here rarely amount to more than bouts of heated verbal barracking as opposed to the unleashing of fists and feet. To explain this further I give you a simple sentence: Uncle Sam versus Japan. Devotees of American-made Harley-Davidson motorcycles often have a pathological loathing of bikes from the land of the Rising Sun (as do some British bike aficionados), although it must be noted that the worldwide influx of Japanese bikes over the past thirty years has provided some stunningly quick donor engines for an array of customised machines, and kept the cafe racer speed-freak ethos of the 1950s astonishingly up to date. Torah Torah Torah!

Japanese motorcycle imports to the USA, Australia and Europe had started piece-meal in the 1950s, but were destined to grow year on year, as Japan's economic infrastructure strengthened. The early oriental offerings sent overseas were predominantly small capacity, cheap run-arounds aimed at the 'transport only' market. As such they were not taken seriously by the lifestyle Biker. These machines were also the brunt of many jokes, which in the main centred around their (arguably) suspect build quality. Because of this, it was thought at the time these imported bikes from the likes of Honda, Suzuki, Kawasaki and Yamaha (the big four) could never catch on. Or could they?

After a decade of continual model re-designs matched with growing race track success, a desire to corner either the quality and/or cult market pushed Honda into launching a key motorbike: The legendary CB750cc K1. This motorbike was, dare I say it, as important to the development and history of the motor cycle as the design classic side-by-side twin cylindered Triumph Bonneville 650cc and 750cc of the 1960s and 1970s, and the V-Twin 1200cc and 1340cc Harley-Davidson Electra-Glides. The late 1960s CB 750cc K1 was an in-line four cylindered machine which sported four gleaming chrome exhaust pipes and was an instant success. Available at that time in a choice of bright red or metallic gold livery, this bike was incredibly fast and symbolised the fact that Honda had finally come of age. They had produced Japan's first 'Super Bike.'

The 1970s saw the equally potent four cylinder Z900cc Kawasaki and this too quickly found an array of devotees among many latter-day Ton-Up Boys. As

such, the oriental dominance of the global motorcycle industry had begun. The British bike industry then slipped into a seemingly irreversible decline due to (i) high inflation which made their machines seem too expensive compared to their Japanese counterparts and (ii) the British bike industry's resistance to change, resulting in their dated designs being unable to successfully compete in an ever-more aggressive market place.

The result, as they say, is history. Despite many 'Smash the Jap Bike' ceremonies which took place at an assortment of Biker rallies throughout the 1970s, over the ensuing decades the Japanese motorcycle industry went from strength to strength – meanwhile, the Milwaukee manufacturers of Messrs Harley and Davidson entered a very bleak period indeed...

chapter siX:

Survival
of
the
Fittest

Just how bleak this period was for Harley-Davidson in the 1970s and early 1980s was vividly brought home to me while on a ride from San Jose to San Francisco one day back in 1984. I was shocked to bear witness to what at that time was an abhorrent abomination: two archetypical Californian Highway Patrol Police motorcyclists (CHiPs) astride a pair of brand new, suitably bedecked, black and white livery police issue Kawasaki 1000cc cycles. Although these bikes were kitted-out in such a way that the untutored would notice no change from the traditional H-D (they sported high cruise-bars, big screens, panniers, wide single seats, foot runners instead of pegs and gold decals), these bikes were *not* Harley-Davidsons, and did *not* boast a magnificent thumping V-Twin motor but a slick and silent in-line four!

In the opening paragraphs of this book I said I would not disclose the make and model of my current motorcycle. Nor am I one of those Bikers who holds the aforementioned unreasoned and pathological loathing for Japanese machinery. However, I must inform you here and now that I have owned an array of oriental offerings since the mid-1970s (along with many European and American bikes), including a big cubed Kawasaki similar to the CHiPs bikes under scrutiny that day in California. I have no problem with motorcycles from the Land of the Rising Sun, far from it, but for a Californian police motorcyclist to be sent out on duty astride a fully sanctioned non-H-D was (and arguably still is) an outrageous travesty!

The root of the problem could in theory be found in facets of Harley-Davidson's (then) ownership. To understand these problems, and why they occurred, we must first go back to before they manifested themselves, to look for the problems at source. I am not about to give you an in-depth model by model history of Harley-Davidson motorcycles however - for that, you'd do better to consult Allan Girdler's book as detailed in the bibliography. Instead I am going to give you the salient points in précis so as to (hopefully) help sign-post what went wrong, where, when and how.

Harley-Davidson are believed to have started producing motorcycles en-mass in 1903, but in actual fact their first models appeared some six years earlier in 1897. Harley are synonymous with the V-Twin engine, although they have produced an assortment of other engine styles in their time including a range of two-strokes, boxer twins, and four pot engines to outline just a few. Nonetheless, it is the ubiquitous range of large cubed V-Twin engines we know and love Harley for. Until 1984, each engine derived its name from the appearance and shape of its given cylinder head. These styles include such engine types as the Knucklehead (1936 to 1947), the Panhead (1948 to 1965) and the Shovelhead (1966 to 1984).

It was during the Shovelhead years that the problems started to compound for the Milwaukee maestros at Harley-Davidson motorcycles. Much of this was primarily due to their forms of funding. As Japanese import sales grew in line with changing consumer patterns, Harley's sales fell off. To counteract this, and raise funds for model development to try to win back their home market, the H-D factory went from being a privately owned corporation to being an (arguably) under-funded public corporation in 1965. This was achieved by the directors/owners selling off around 50% of their shares to the public sector in order to finance the Shovelhead powered range of machines that it was believed and hoped would restore them to their former glory.

This was not enough to save the factory's fortunes though. After much internal and political wrangling, it was decided in 1969 (the year *Easy Rider* was released) to sell Harley-Davidson motorcycles to a large company, which resulted in the marque becoming a wholly owned subsidiary of the AMF (American Machine & Foundry) group. At that time, AMF were primarily known for their involvement in the ten-pin bowling industry. To many die-hard bike lovers, this belittled the illustrious name of Harley-Davidson, especially as AMF started to incorporate their initials within the petrol tank decals of the bikes they produced.

AMF then moved some of Harley-Davidson's production processes to Pennsylvania, which according to the aforementioned anti-AMF lobby, brought about a decline in build quality. Sales did not reflect this however, as in 1975 in excess of 75,000 Harley-Davidson motorcycles were produced and sold, an all-time H-D high. To be fair, AMF invested heavily in Harley's development after this, and despite year-on-year declining sales, replaced the 74 cube (1200cc) standard Shovelhead engine with an 80 cube (1340cc) version in 1978. This engine then became the power-plant behind all new big twin Harley's and, as an ex-AMF 80 cube Wide Glide owner, I can confirm that this unit really did deliver the goods. But Harley-Davidson's fortunes were further hindered by the American recession which hit in the early 1980s, leaving the expensive H-D's struggling to compete with the profusion of oriental bikes which were available in an array of styles and sizes.

By increasing their model range and reducing their profit margins via the rationalisation of production procedures, AMF managed to hold their own in the face of such daunting competition - but at a price. Firstly, reducing production costs to keep unit prices down further fuelled the speculation about declining build quality; secondly, many within the AMF hierarchy believed the production of Harley-Davidson motorcycles at nominal profit was severely hindering their corporate growth in other areas, as their bikes were still more costly than their Japanese counterparts. Bearing all this in mind, was it any wonder that the CHiPs riders I encountered outside San Jose in 1982 were astride Kawasakis? Fortunately, evolution would see to it that things would change in Harley-Davidson's favour, and ultimately restore their credibility and quality.

In 1981 another change of ownership for Harley-

Davidson was instigated which was complete by the following year. Arguably over-stretched by motorcycle manufacturing, AMF elected to accept a management buy-out package for their motorcycle arm from a group which included members of the original Davidson family. This was a happy parting of the ways though and the new consortium were elated. As a note here however, it must be mentioned that had it not been for the AMF ownership era, it is most unlikely that Harley would have ever made it through the 1970s.

The new consortium behind Harley had big plans, and secured enough funding to develop a new style engine that would take their beloved cycles through to the 21st century. Thanks to the diligence of their research and development experts, by 1984 the new engine was complete. Although occasionally called a Flathead in an attempt to follow the H-D tradition of naming engines after cylinder-head shapes, this unit is far more commonly known as the Evolution (or Evo for short), because of its internal departure from what had gone before. For this truly was a Darwin-esque engine progression which symbolised Harley-Davidson's natural selection and organic ethos of survival of the fittest. Still being an 80 cube (1340cc) V-Twin, this engine is still in the acceptable Harley-Davidson genre and, as an engineer, I must say is a most marvellous motor (also available in 883cc and 1200cc for 'Sportster' models).

Motorcycles powered by the Evolution engine first went on sale in 1984 in a range of models which, apart from the Tourers and Sportsters, are generically referred to as Factory Customs. A minority saw this new engine type as being too radical and initially snubbed it via the play on words of 'see no Evo, hear no Evo'. However, the popularity of the Evolution-powered Harley soon became so widespread that waiting lists developed for them the world over. Ever conscious of the build quality debacle which had plagued AMF, however, the new owners of H-D refused to be rushed so they allowed the waiting lists to remain while they employed and trained new staff and opened additional production and assembly lines. This approach resulted in increased quality and production, a greater workforce and an ever-increasing range of motorcycle types to house the new style engine (my favourite being the Softail Custom). Happily, within a couple of years, demand also grew for the new Evo FXR-P and FLH-P, both of which were specifically aimed at the police market - they have since superseded all that went before.

Quick not to miss a trick, Japanese motorcycle manufacturers have produced an array of V-Twinned Harley look-a-like Factory Customs since the 1990s aimed at cashing in on the Evo's success. Some of these have been exceptionally good although I must still point out that if you want a Coke, buy a Coke. However, one area where Japanese factory custom motorcycles have excelled in latter years is in the retro sphere. A good example of this is the Kawasaki 1100cc Zephyr. Based around their mid-1970s Z900cc, this machine looks good with its chromed instruments and exhausts, and oozes an air of quality reminiscent of a bygone era. Japanese engines have also appeared in a fantastic range of hand-crafted custom bikes, although for my money, the best of these are in the British-led Street-Fighter style - truly awesome. The Big four also do well in the field of sports performance bikes, although here the Italian manufacturer of Ducati is, in my opinion, the Daddy. As sports bikes are a topic for a different publication though, we'll leave the speed-freak machines here and return to the stalwart lifestyle Biker.

The chronicling of an archetypical Biker image since 1980 has become more and more difficult due to the ever-expanding and diverse pool from which Bikers draw influence. Suffice to say, there is now no one specific image associated with Cycle culture, but a hybrid of many which encompasses all the elements previously mentioned in this book plus an array of others. These can on occasion include Punk-styled spiky hair, cropped Skinhead cuts and even, in some instances, Rastafarian-styled dreadlocks. Long and wild or mullet-styled hair prevails as the most popular choice though, along with beards. Since the 1950s, Bikers (male and female) have pierced their ears, but today some have taken this further and adopted aspects of body piercing such as multi-ear piercing, nose and nipple, and other facial piercings to enhance the identity and image they wish to create.

Body piercing started to creep into Biker Culture around 1985 when this practice joined the traditional tattoo under the (then) new umbrella term of body art. Tattoos have been big with Bikers of both sexes since the 1940s. These days they not only range from the predictable club decals, bike badges (particularly Harley-Davidson), and 'Live to Ride - Ride to Live' logos (which often incorporate demonic looking bike and rider designs) of yesteryear, but now may also include Celtic artwork and/or Maori-styled tribal warrior graphics in thick dense lines of swirling black ink.

Musically, too, the 21st Century Biker has no limitations of what he/she may or may not listen to, which has created the most refreshingly diverse range of sounds imaginable at Biker events the world over. For not only do these include all the styles of music this book has listed (along with their updates), but are equally likely to include offerings from the likes of the Sex Pistols, The Pogues, and even the Prodigy. I have even seen live performances from the Skinhead/Scooterist Ska Reggae band Bad Manners at two large-scale Biker events I've attended, where it must be said that on each occasion, they went down a storm. But if it's tradition that you want, and should you ever venture to London on your travels, do yourself a favour and make your way to the recently re-opened Ace Cafe which has been resurrected by a devoted team to its former egg and chip chompin' petrol-headed Rock & Roll glory.

Epilogue:

Enough said?

My solace in the introduction to this book for the necessarily skin deep surface scratching of the Biker story that this work proffers comes from an analogy I heard while in Chicago back in 1987. It emerged from a wise old Bro who sat astride a Harley 45 sucking a pipe amidst a gathering of trendy young things on Yama-haka-suzis. Several of these young bucks walked up to the old timer whose face was barely visible beneath an amazing matt of grey whiskers, and asked why he rode such an old Hog and what was he all about? They were trying to score points off him, but once he'd spoken, their silent respect was deafening. For after the question was asked, the Biker behind the beard slowly pulled his pipe from his mouth, straightened his back, and spoke in a deep, soft, thought provoking tone.

"If you have to ask the question, then you won't understand the answer. But if its an understanding you want, I'll give you a word picture. Cycle life is like a deep flowing river with tributaries going off in all directions. Some of these flow into it, feeding it, and some flow away, carving paths through new ground. Yet they all rely on Mother river for their being, for that is where they can mix with other waters before flowing in the direction the forces that effect them dictate. If you skim a flat faced pebble across the top, you can at least understand the way the surface of the river works by watching the many ripples that appear, but to know what lies below an individual ripple you must dive in and feel the water beneath it, and allow yourself to be taken by this water to wherever you may end."

I believe this book to be a skimming stone, and its content metaphoric ripples. The diversity and depth of the international Biker movement can be directly attributed to the wide-ranging appeal and freedom it perpetuates, along with the varied cross section of people the name Biker can encompass. Biking was always more than a rebellious interruption of the growing up process, and is a truly liberating way of life.

To observe is to envy, to be involved is to understand.

Ride Free.

Gary Charles.

Bibliography

(In chronological order by title)

AWOPBOPALOOBOP ALOPBAMBOOM by N. Cohn, Weidenfield & Nicolson, 1969

Working Class Youth Culture by Mungham & Pearson, Routledge, 1976

Classic Motorcycles by V. Willoughby, Hamlyn Publishing, 1977

The Teds by Steel-Perkins & Smith, Travelling Light Publications, 1979

British Beat Groups of the Sixties by Cross, Kendall & Farren, Omnibus Press, 1980

Bikers by M. Harris, Faber & Faber, 1985

You'll Never Be Sixteen Again by P. Everett, BBC Publications, 1986

(The) Best Years of Their Lives – The National Service Experience, 1945-1963 by T. Royal, Michael Joseph Ltd, 1986

The Sociology of Youth by S. Frith., Causeway Press, 1986
Harley-Davidson Buyer's Guide by A. Girdler, Motorbooks, 1986

Cafe Racers by M. Clay, Osprey Publishing, 1988

Only In America by A. Woodiwiss, University Press, 1993

Rock and Roll: A Social History by P. Friedlander, Westview Press, 1996

Scooter Boys by Gareth Brown, 6th Edition, Independent Music Press, 2001

Skins by Gavin Watson, Independent Music Press, 2001

Almost Grown: The Rise of Rock by J. Miller, William Heinmann 1999

SKINS By Gavin Watson
Introduction by Ted Polhemus

Perhaps one of the most reviled yet misunderstood of all the youth subcultures, the skinhead look originated back in the 60s as a simple fashion statement. Sartorially proud of their working class roots, the original skinhead was a multi-cultural, politically broad-minded and fashion-aware individual. Favourite music was reggae, soul and ska and key artists included Desmond Dekker, Max Romeo and The Pyramids. Their choice of immaculate clothing and invariably Dr. Martens boots was the ultimate anti-fashion statement and a badge of both power and pride. Above all else, genuine skinheads were obsessed with their presentation.

The 70s saw the look adopted by the scurge of right-wing extremists and for many years was a fashion pariah. However, towards the end of the 90s, the closely cropped look has been championed by a whole new generation of high profile celebrities, including David Beckham and Ewan McGregor, bringing skinhead style back into the mainstream once again.

Gavin Watson's critically acclaimed photography of late 70s and 80s skinheads perfectly captures a snapshot of this unique youth culture. The scores of black and white shots offer a fascinating glimpse into a skinhead community that was multi-cultural, tightly knit and above all else, fiercely proud of their look. These are classic photographs of historical value.

FHM
"There once was the time when the sight of a young man with a Number One all over struck horror into middle-class England. And Gavin Watson's photos will show you why: the blank stares, 18-hole Doc Martens and home-made tattoos of a 'real' skin are as far from David Beckham's bovine, non-threatening mug as it's possible to get. The world these photographs depict - smoking on trains, buying vinyl down the market - is all captured in minute detail here. And a good thing too. Whether you were there or not there's an undeniable pull to these pictures, making *Skins* an oddly compelling tome."

THE TIMES
"A modern classic."

128 pgs   75 B&W Photos   ISBN: 0-9539942-1-X   £9.99 + £2.00 p+p

also available from

I INDEPENDENT MUSIC PRESS I

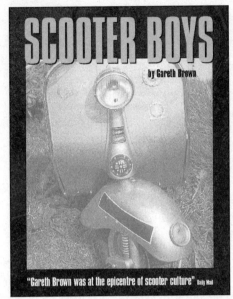

"Gareth Brown was at the epicentre of scooter culture" *Daily Mail*

SCOOTER BOYS By Gareth Brown

From the post-punk, massed Mod revival of the 1970s, there emerged an almost organic cultural collective - Scooter Boys. With an underlying musical focus on Northern Soul and R&B, these scooter boys developed a passion for steamy all nighters, fuelled by a fast, absorbing and intrinsically nomadic lifestyle.

They gathered in their thousands at an array of coastal resorts all over the British Isles (and beyond) for all weekend parties, making their own rules and their own enemies. The cultural icon at the epicentre of this phenomenon were the Italian motor-scooters which mobilised this unique way of life.

In the 1990s, yet another string was added to the bow of scooter culture, courtesy of artists such as Oasis, Ocean Colour Scene and Cast. These bands, along with the already 'scooter-credible' Paul Weller, helped fuel a new generation of scooter-loving individuals.

Gareth Brown's youth culture classic *Scooter Boys* is now reprinted proudly on Independent Music Press. Brown is widely regarded as the leading world authority on scooter culture. His writings on scooter culture have been published in magazines throughout the world and a signed scooter he once owned sold for £10,000 in Japan.

NEW INSIGHT MAGAZINE
"Ah, the scooter - paradoxical symbol of post-war austerity and affluence, and bete-noire of deckchair insurers everywhere. Gareth Brown's history of the various overlapping subcultures that have attached themselves to Vespas, Lambrettas and other small-wheeled motorbikes for nearly half a century occasionally comes across as a tad rushed. But the ex-editor of *Scootering* magazine's knowledge of and commitment to a fascinating and photogenic subject is clear from the kick off - and some of the classic models on display must rank amongst the greatest achievements of 20th Century design. If you were ever involved in any of the scenes described here, there's probably about a fifty fifty chance you're somewhere in one of the many photos. If you weren't, even a brief flick through this book will have you thinking "Maybe that's the life for me..?" Till you get to the photo of Buster Bloodvessel on page 66, that is."

THE DAILY MAIL
"Gareth Brown was centre stage in the rebirth of one of Britain's longest surviving youth cultures."

128 pages   100 B&W Photos   ISBN 0-9539942-0-1   £9.99 + £2.00 p+p

MOBY: REPLAY - HIS LIFE AND TIMES

This is the first and only book on Moby and draws from exclusive and lengthy interviews conducted over the last seven years with Moby himself. It is the definitive look at Moby's remarkable life. Every aspect of his seminal career is covered at length, from his much reported Christian, vegan, non-drinking, non-drug-taking stance to his subsequent metamorphosis into the hard-drinking party animal he is today.

Embracing skate punk to New York house, thrash metal to chilled ambience, soundtracks to downtempo blues, few artists have reflected the eclectic nature of our times quite like Moby. Also, few artists of the modern era have been immersed in so many different scenes and genres - this book also details the genesis of the underground dance scene and its subsequent evolution through a multitude of subgenres.

From the first rave hits to the multi-million selling album *Play*, Moby's music soundtracks every walk of life. *Moby: Replay - His Life and Times* documents this compelling climb to the top of the music charts and offers the inside take on the enigma behind that success.

By Martin James
208 pages *including 8pgs b/w plates*
£9.99 + £1.00 p+p

STEREOPHONICS: HIGH TIMES & HEADLINES

This is the first comprehensive and unauthorised biography of the most popular UK three-piece since the Jam. *High Times And Headlines* follows their rocket rise to fame, analysing their musical achievements in detail while exploring the 'neighbourhood gang' mentality that keeps their feet firmly on the ground. It details the breaks that brought them their recording contract, their healthily cynical attitude to the music business in general and their stunning live performances.

Since signing to Richard Branson's V2 record label, Stereophonics - Kelly Jones, Richard Jones and Stuart Cable - have sold millions of records, picked up hatfuls of awards and sold out some of the biggest venues in the world, including Cardiff's cavernous Millenium Stadium. The book is now updated to include full coverage of the band's continued globe-trotting success and rise to world fame. 2001's brilliantly accomplished third album, *Just Enough Education To Perform*, confirmed Stereophonics' status as Britain's biggest band, silencing the doubters and achieving a level of commercial success that most acts could only dream of.

By Mike Black
144 pages, *Illustrated throughout with scores of colour and b/w photos*
£9.99 + £2.00 p+p

TRAVIS: CLOSER EVERY YEAR

This is the first ever biography of the band who in twelve short months have come out of nowhere to claim every prize in the UK music industry.

Their brand of spiritual and lyrical rock struck such a chord with the public that in the first week of 2000, their remarkable second album, *The Man Who* returned to the No. 1 spot it had occupied several times throughout 1999, and in the process notched up an incredible 1.8 million sales.

Travis: Closer Every Year tells the roller-coaster story of the band who met at Glasgow School of Art in 1990, spending years trawling the underground gig circuit, before a performance on *Later With Jools Holland* caused a record company dash to sign them.

By Mike Black
144 pages, *Illustrated throughout with scores of colour and b/w photos*
£9.99 + £2.00 p+p

WE CAN BE HEROES: LIFE ON TOUR WITH DAVID BOWIE

In 1978, Sean Mayes toured the world with David Bowie. Travelling first class and performing each night with one of the world's greatest rock stars at the height of his fame was an amazing experience - fortunately, Sean had the foresight to document it. Here, for the first time in complete book form, Sean's tour diary is presented; a blow by blow record of how it felt to be part of a real rock circus.

Providing page after page of fascinating insights into life on the road with Bowie, Sean's account is a unique travelogue, a must for any Bowie fan or, indeed, anyone interested in life on a sell-out world tour. Also includes a full tour chronology and previously unpublished photos from Sean's personal archive.

By Sean Mayes
160 Pages including 8pgs b/w plates
£7.99 + £1.00 p+p

RHYMING & STEALING: A HISTORY OF THE BEASTIE BOYS

The first biographical attempt to document the band's metamorphosis from their initial incarnation as Greenwich Village punk rockers, through their days as rap's biggest pop stars and on to their present status as all-conquering multi-media coolest people in rock.

This volatile and fascinating history examines their beer-soaked rise to global infamy, the phenomenal commercial success of the *Licensed To Ill* album, as well as their years in the wilderness and the critical rehabilitation afforded to them during the *Ill Communication* period.

With comprehensive accounts of the band's entire career, including their many side-projects such as the Grand Royale label, their magazine and clothing range, as well as their championing of the Tibetan Freedom cause, *Rhyming & Stealing* is the first full history of one of modern music's most important and influential bands.

By Angus Batey
208pgs including 8pgs b/w plates
£9.99 + £1.00p+p

IAN MCCULLOCH - KING OF COOL

Ian McCulloch was born with the gift of a golden voice. He was the Bowie freak who dreamed of rock stardom and found it as the outspoken leader of Echo And The Bunnymen, arguably the most brilliant and bewildering band in recent pop history.

For ten years it was a feast of rock 'n' roll hedonism. Then, as McCulloch's self-confessed ego became increasingly bloated, the band imploded. Against the odds, Echo And The Bunnymen were to return triumphantly in the late nineties as unlikely godfathers to an entire generation of post-Britpop contenders.

By Mick Middles
208pgs including 8pgs b/w plates
£9.99 + £1.00p+p

PRODIGY - THE FAT OF THE LAND

The official book to accompany the global No. 1 album. The Prodigy are the world's biggest selling hard dance act - with over five million records sold and Top Ten singles in over thirty countries, they are both internationally successful and critically revered. This official book reveals, in entirely the band's own words, the thinking behind such ground-breaking releases as 'Firestarter' and 'Breathe', and gives an insider's view on their remarkable live show and life in The Prodigy.

With dozens of unpublished colour and duotone shots of the band backstage, live, in the studio

and at home, *The Fat Of The Land* is a unique and essential visual insight into The Prodigy, as well as a stunning snapshot of a band that have single-handedly redefined modern music.

By Martin Roach
112pgs
£12.99 + £1.50p+p

SHAUN RYDER: HAPPY MONDAYS, BLACK GRAPE & OTHER TRAUMAS

Formed from the fringes of juvenile criminality in Swinton in 1984, Happy Mondays established themselves, not so much as a band in the traditional sense, but as a swirling vortex of wild hedonism. Fuelled by endless tales of petty thievery, drug dealing, pill popping, skag smoking, car smashing, purse nabbing, liberty taking and rogue-ish near anarchy, Happy Mondays careered uncontrollably through the heart of the late eighties Madchester rave scene before finally imploding in spectacular fashion.

This book chronicles this story and details how, from the ashes of the Mondays, self-confessed heroin addict and ex-postman, Shaun Ryder defied all the odds to emerge triumphant as the front man of Black Grape, arguably the only band who fulfilled the potential laid down by their flawed predecessors.

By Mick Middles
208pgs including 8pgs b/w plates
£9.99 + £1.00p+p

DIARY OF A ROCK 'N' ROLL STAR - IAN HUNTER

Widely regarded as the first rock autobiography and universally acclaimed as one of the finest ever insights into life on the road, this best-selling title is now re-printed for the first time in 15 years. Revealing the rigours of Mott The Hoople's enigmatic frontman, this is a landmark publication.

Q magazine simply called it "the greatest music book ever written."

By Ian Hunter
160pgs with 28 photo's
£8.95 + £1.00p+p

OASIS - ROUND THEIR WAY

This is the first major biography of Oasis, the multi-million selling Manchester band led by the Gallagher brothers Noel and Liam.

Round Their Way follows the Oasis story from their unlikely beginnings as The Rain to their present day status as the most talked about band in the world. Includes full details of the sibling rivalry between Noel and Liam, their family life in Manchester, their infamous rock 'n' roll reputation, and includes the most comprehensive Oasis discography ever published.

By Mick Middles
128pgs including 8pgs b/w
£9.99 + £1.00p+p

POP BOOK NUMBER ONE - STEVE GULLICK

This fine collection of Steve Gullick's work from 1988-1995 captures the key figures in alternative world music. With rare and unpublished shots of Nirvana, Pearl Jam, Hole, Blur, Bjork, and many more, this is the most accomplished photo history of alternative music. *The Times* called it "one of the most beautiful and necessary books about 1990's pop and rock" whilst *Melody Maker* said "So stylish, so rockin'."

By Steve Gullick
112pgs with 108 duo-tone photo's
£12.95 + £1.50p+p

THE BUZZCOCKS - THE COMPLETE HISTORY

The fully authorised biography of one of the prime movers of the

HOW TO ORDER ANY OF THESE BOOKS

PLEASE SEND £STERLING CASH, CHEQUES, POSTAL ORDERS
OR INTERNATIONAL MONEY ORDERS PAYABLE TO:

I. M. P. LTD.

and send your payments to:

I.M.P,
P.O.BOX 14691,
LONDON SE1 2ZA

Please allow 28 days for delivery

*Visit us at **www.impbooks.com***

for full details of all our music titles

and information on our new fiction label,

I.M.P. FICTION